1-2-3 got my

JOB

A guide to get YOU the job of your dreams

BY RICARDO TRINIDAD

1-2-3 got my JOB

This book cannot help you get a job as a brain surgeon when you have never been to medical school. After you read this book, employers will not magically start knocking at your door, begging you to work for them. Quite the opposite, in fact. 1-2-3 GOT MY JOB will give you the tools to go knocking on doors and find work that is fulfilling, interesting, and rewarding.

Published by Fig Factor Media, LLC
www.figfactormedia.com

Cover Design & Layout by Juan Pablo Ruiz

Printed in the United States of America

ISBN: 978-1-7330635-8-6
Library of Congress # 2019912955

**FIG
FACTOR
MEDIA**

Table of Contents

ACKNOWLEDGEMENTS 4

PREFACE: WHY WORK IS SO IMPORTANT...........................5

BELIEVE IN YOU 9

YOUR DREAM JOB 19

RESEARCHING FOR YOUR NEW JOB................................21

THINK LIKE AN ENTREPRENEUR 27

MARKETING YOURSELF 30

THE INTERVIEW 41

I DIDN'T GET THE JOB. NOW WHAT?.............................50

I GOT MY JOB. NOW WHAT? 53

ABOUT THE AUTHOR 58

ACKNOWLEDGMENTS

Writing this book was a pleasure, and most of it was written sitting in the window seat of various flights. Every time I was away on business, I would write. Being away makes a person miss their family, and so I would like to thank my wife Dianna, my daughters Brigitte and Dianeli and my son, Antonio. I would also like to thank my parents, Ruby and Julio Trinidad, for instilling in me a great work ethic at a very young age. Finally, I would like to thank the people that helped me with this book, including my sister, Christina Trinidad, Kira Henschel, Michele Kelly and my dear, long-time friend who has been an inspiration to me and many others, Jackie Camacho. Jackie believed in this book and stayed on me to complete it.

Most of all, I would like to thank you, the reader, who has decided to move forward with your life and read this book. You are about to learn all kinds of creative ways to get the job of your dreams.

Before jumping into this book, or anything you do, it's really important to enter into the spirit of this book with the expectation that it will help deliver the job of your dreams to you. You must start believing this now, and don't look back, because it will work.

Thank you.

PREFACE
Why Work is so Important

Many young people in our country, particularly those from households where parents have relatively little education and therefore mostly blue-collar jobs, do not have the tools, or meager access to the tools, for finding a fulfilling job. Ricardo Trinidad's book provides a timely, concise, and easy to follow step-by-step approach to finding a "dream" job for students.

This short and compact book provides students— high school or college—a sort of "worksheet" for how to seek, apply, and hopefully find a "dream" job. It targets finding employment in the private sector, rather than in non-profits. Nonetheless, in the span of an hour, a student can read the book and get very good advice on how to go about securing his/her "dream" job. Mr. Trinidad's 30-plus years of working in the private sector and thereafter starting and growing his own company, provide the reader with a wealth of valuable information.

The reader will first be introduced to a "motivational" section where a distinction is made about jobs that you "do" as compared to jobs where you "be." A mindset is introduced to show the reader that any obstacle can be overcome, and the primary obstacle is for all of us to cease on our narratives about why we can't do something. The reader is led into a deep introspection of how we all have developed narratives about our lives that hold us back from pursuing our "dream" job. Though higher education is important and certainly required for some jobs, it is not imperative for securing your "dream" job. Fundamental to the job search is that you have to "believe in yourself."

Sections of this book direct readers to create worksheets for answering important questions about what and how "dream" jobs are attainable. Readers should do the worksheets, for they help to debunk negative self-narratives. Additionally, some of the exercises contribute to a better self-understanding of what a "dream" job will mean—e.g., how do I know what my "dream" job would be.

This book chronicles and explains the process for finding your "dream" job—from doing the research of what is out there, to crafting your resume, how to knocking on doors for an interview, preparing for an interview, having an interview, following up on the interview, what to do if you're not successful in your interview, what to do if you are successful in your interview, and finally, what to do to stand out and excel in your job.

This book can also be helpful to parents, for they can provide the catalyst to their children in their pursuit of employment.

Ricardo Trinidad has written a book that will serve as a life-changing read to some youth. His contribution will have a positive impact on our communities, for the aggregation of individual achievements translates to more vibrant and cohesive communities.

Yo soy,

Enrique E. Figueroa, Ph.D., *Emeritus,* Associate Professor
Dept. of Urban Planning
University of Wisconsin, Milwaukee

BELIEVE IN YOU

What is your story? Ever since we were children, a story has been building inside of us. Our parents may have been the very first to plant the seeds of our stories. We may have had the story reinforced by teachers, relatives, classmates, siblings, and others.

Soon, we start to tell ourselves these stories or make up new stories. Then these stories become our beliefs and go in many different directions.

Some of these stories or beliefs are helpful and positive, such as "I am smart" or "I never get sick." On the other hand, some stories that are now beliefs can cause us great harm. We can believe we are dumb, unattractive, lazy, no good, or worse.

As an entrepreneur who started my own business, and has been in sales for 30 years I have met thousands of people. Every one of them has a story to tell and a system of beliefs and values. You do, too.

The idea here is that the beliefs we have about ourselves are only stories we tell. The truth, is in your purest form, you are whole, perfect, and amazing. Please read these words again and say them out loud:

- I am whole.
- I am perfect.
- I am amazing.

What does this have to do with getting a job? Everything!

To get the job of your dreams, you must first believe you can.

You also have to stop telling stories that keep you from doing anything in life you really want. This one thing can be the defining difference between success and failure.

How about the stories that race through a guy's mind when he sees a beautiful girl and without saying hello, dismisses the whole idea of talking to her by thinking, "I don't stand a chance." "My nose is too big." "I am too old or too young, too short, too tall," … or any other story he can think of that stops him from doing the thing he really wants to do.

What stories have you told yourself today that have held you back from doing something?

Finding your dream job is a lot like finding that perfect person and having the courage to go up and introduce yourself. It may seem intimidating, but unless you tell yourself the right story, you might not even try.

What do you believe is holding you back from getting your dream job or any job right now?

Below, or on a separate sheet of paper, write down all the things that are stopping you from getting that job.

Don't leave out anything that may be holding you back.

Do Not Skip This Step!

List all the reasons below.

....

....

....

....

....

....

Let me give you some examples of people who had some major obstacles and overcame them, so it will be easier to tell the difference between an obstacle you can overcome or if the "reason" is a story you are telling yourself.

Tony Melendez

Being a guitar player, one of my favorite people who put aside his obstacles is Tony Melendez. Tony Melendez is a professional guitarist, songwriter, and minister who lives in Branson, Missouri. Tony's band, appropriately (or inappropriately) is called "Toe Jam" and plays hundreds of shows per year all over the world. The band has even played for Pope John Paul II!

Tony's obstacle was that he was born without arms. Check out Tony Melendez at www.tony-melendez.com. Now, say you knew Tony when he was a young boy and he told you he wanted to play guitar, but can't because he had no arms. What would you say? Was he telling a story of limiting belief or does he merely have an obstacle to overcome?

Cornel Hrisca Munn

Still having trouble deciding if your reasons are stories or mere obstacles? How about Cornel Hrisca Munn? Cornel was born in Romania in 1991 without forearms and with a severely disfigured leg. He was taken from the hospital where he was born and placed in an orphanage.

Cornel ended up in a room with many unwanted babies and was given little milk and food so that he would not be a burden for long. Instead, he was rescued by a British couple who adopted him. After consulting with doctors, Cornel's parents decided to amputate his disfigured leg and fit it with a prosthetic one.

Now, what kind of stories could young Cornel tell himself at this point? Cornel ended up having a desire to play the drums and while in middle school, he asked his music teacher if he could play the drums in the school band. His teacher told him it would be better to find a one-hand-friendly instrument. This only made Cornel more determined to become a drummer.

Cornel continued practicing drums and joined the school's jazz band. He eventually attended Oxford University, one of the most prestigious universities in the world.

This gifted musician also runs a charity that raises money to help disabled children. Check out Cornel's story at www.thecorneltrust.co.uk/cornels-story.

Bethany Hamilton

Bethany Hamilton was, and still is, a champion surfer, even after an encounter in 2003 with a

Fourteen-foot-shark that ripped her arm off.

I think Bethany has a special kind of courage. She is an ideal role model for many people, since she certainly lives out her passion.

One year after the shark attack, Bethany won her first National Championship in surfing. Today, Bethany is involved with numerous charitable organizations working with young amputees to help them overcome limiting beliefs.

Danny Glover

Danny Glover is an elite Hollywood actor who was diagnosed with both epilepsy and dyslexia at the age of fifteen. Danny was able to overcome his handicaps to attend college and become a leading actor and political activist for peace and human rights.

* * * * *

Did you know there is a list online of college dropout billionaires? The top twenty of this group are worth more than the top twenty with PhDs by about three times. So, cross off education—or lack thereof—as something that is holding you back. Sure, education is important, but never allow a lack of education to restrict your dreams. It's just a story.

Sir Richard Branson

You can learn just about anything by reading. One of my favorite entrepreneurs is Sir Richard Branson. Sir Branson is the owner of Virgin Group, a holding company of over four hundred businesses, including Virgin Cellular and Virgin Airways.

At the beginning, things were tough for Sir Branson. He was dyslexic and dropped out of school at the age of sixteen. Today, Sir Richard Branson is listed as one of *Forbes'* richest business-men in the world, with his own private island in the British Virgin Islands.

Do your own research and find your own examples. The world is full of successful people who do not have degrees or who had to leave school early.

What stories did Tony, Cornel, Sir Richard, Bethany, and Danny tell themselves? What stories are you telling yourself?

Look again at the list of things you wrote down that may be holding you back. Is "no jobs" or "lack of jobs" on your list? Guess what?! That should not be on the list because all around you, people are working and there are plenty of jobs.

When reviewing your list, please be honest with yourself in defining your reasons for not having a job. Is it a story or just an obstacle?

Please remember you have the power to overcome any obstacle as long as you believe you can. If you have been telling yourself stories that do not benefit you, it's time to stop and replace those stories with one that shows you believe in YOU!

14

How about this story?

- I can succeed!
- All that is possible to anyone is possible to me.
- I am successful.
- I do succeed, for I am full of the power of success.

So, how can you replace an old, limiting story or belief with a new one?

First, realize how much these stories have cost you, not only in money, but in the total enjoyment of your life. Maybe you wanted to try out for a sport, play an instrument or ask someone special to a dance. Really visualize and feel what the stories throughout your life have cost you.

Belief and Self-Worth

One of the ways people limit their opportunities is by having low self-worth. I have been a witness to this and have felt unworthy of things. Where do these feelings come from and how do you get rid of them?

Success and worthiness starts with a belief deep inside that says I am good, I can do this, I am special and I have talents and things to offer and share. How do you get that feeling of success to start shining through your entire being so that people notice it all around you?

Everyone has special talents. Getting those talents to shine and making them known to others can be done through something as simple as volunteering.

Volunteering is giving, and giving is a powerful energy. Something special happens when you give. When you give you are actually receiving, and this receiving energy is so strong it can bring about major changes in the beliefs you carry about yourself.

How much money would you like to make? If you had your dream job, how much would you be earning? What other benefits would come from that work?

Money brings out all sorts of emotions and many people have extremely limiting beliefs about it. Our parents may have told us things that led us to believe that money is scarce or "does not grow on trees" ... or they may have spent everything they made and then some ... or they saved everything they made and sacrificed any enjoyment of it.

These beliefs often stay with us for the rest of our lives. Maybe some of it was good financial advice. However, unless you think these beliefs really apply to you, you may need to build a different or new relationship with money so that money works for you.

What story are you telling yourself right now and what do you think people like Tony Melendez, Cornel Munn, and Sir Richard Branson are telling themselves? All things are possible when you believe in yourself and your self-worth first. You are worth it!

* * * * *

Look at your list again. How many of the things you wrote down are stories? How many are obstacles to be overcome?

When you want to change anything in your life, you need to first realize how much the story or limiting belief is costing you, not only in terms of money, but in total enjoyment of life.

Really visualize and feel what the realities of these stories have cost you throughout your life. If this makes you feel uncomfortable, you are doing it right. Think of lost opportunities for happiness. Think of bad decisions based on false stories. Add up the months or years you have been holding yourself back.

If you can make the emotional connection to these stories and really feel their weight, you can make the change.

Forgiveness

Everyone makes mistakes, but not everyone forgives. That can hold back lots of successes. Forgive yourself and anyone else you might be blaming for anything. If you are blaming a parent, or former teacher or sibling, former employer, or anybody for anything—the time to stop is now. It is all on you—and up to you.

Over the years, I have met people who were beaten by their parents, raped by a sibling, molested by a trusted family member, cheated on, and even had someone murder a family member. Many of these people were able to forgive the person who caused them so much pain; some actually apologized to the person for making them the scapegoat for all their problems. Now that is powerful.

You are the only one with the power to change everything and anything about your life. Remember, you are perfect, whole, and amazing. Only stories make you anything less. If you can forgive, you can forget the old stories and start telling new ones. Your life can be a blank page—starting today.

This is Important!

Stop here and take out a blank sheet of paper, or use the space on the next page to write. Ask yourself not what you want **to do**, but what you want **to be**.

Write out your new marvelous story of who you want to be. Include your ten best characteristics. Make your new story big and beautiful. Create goals worthy of the amazing person you really are.

Don't leave out any details about what you want to be. You are the architect of your life. This is *your* plan for *your* life, so don't share it with anyone else. It's yours! Post it so you can see it in the morning and at night before you go to sleep. Use it as a screensaver on your phone or computer. Get as excited as you can be about this. It's not a plan unless you write it out.

Try this (and most of all, feel the release of tension associated with the pain)

1. I forgive (Name) for the pain they have caused me.
2. I now live my life free from that pain (Name) caused me.
3. I love and honor myself, for I am worthy and open to all good things.

There can be no obstacle that can keep you away from the new life you want.

My New Life Story — This is Who I Want to BE

....
....
....
....
....
....

YOUR DREAM JOB

What is your dream job? The keyword is *dream*. When dreaming, you are giving yourself the freedom to allow limitless possibilities and outcomes without concern of how, where, or why. The art of dreaming connects you to your higher self, where all things are possible.

I have found that talking to people about their dream job can be difficult. There are virtually limitless choices when it comes to work, but most people don't give themselves the freedom to explore all the options. If they do, many times they quickly switch to critical thinking or add fear to the equation, which quickly shoots down their dream job.

It is really important not to let this happen. Sometimes it's hard not to worry about how you will end up with your dream job. Guess what? Worrying is not your job! Your job is dreaming—so dream big and dream often.

Your dream job choices are limitless and ONLY limited by your imagination. How about becoming a professional waterslide tester, chocolate taste-tester, luxury-bed tester, pearl diver, oil rig diver, Stanley Cup keeper, or how about a professional snuggler?

Yes, these are all real jobs, fulfilling someone's dream and calling in life. I personally could go for being the Stanley Cup keeper.

The types of jobs are limitless and the only thing that separates them from dull jobs is imagination.

STOP!

Get out a piece of paper or use the next page and start writing out your list of dream jobs. Not only the job itself, but get detailed and include the size company, where it should be located, if it is new or well-established. What is the culture of the company like? Why would you want to work at this place? The better and more detailed you can be about the work you dream of doing, the more quickly you can find your dream job!

Try these affirmations:

1. My dream job is available to me now.
2. My perfect dream job reveals itself to me.
3. I am grateful for my new dream job.

RESEARCHING YOUR DREAM JOB

Now that you have let go of all the reasons you "can't," and you've dreamt your dreams and focused in on the job you want, it's time to start looking for it. Today, with the internet, finding your dream job has never been easier. There are a number of ways you can find your new employer. Use a search engine, of course, but search tools can also be limiting. Set up Google Alerts about your dream job industry. Get creative!

Trade Magazines

Trade magazines are a great source of information. There are thousands of publications about every imaginable industry or field of business. Most have free subscriptions.

Trade magazines offer specific insights into the type of business you might be dreaming of and are a great source of current information for researching your own interview questions.

Every industry offers a trade magazine, including underwear, onions, pizza, parking, rocket science, banking, etc. You get the idea.

Free subscription forms for trade magazines will ask you for a company name, address, email, phone number, and other marketing information. Don't worry. Just fill out the application. If you need to make up a company name, go for it. Typically, you won't get turned down for a subscription. Do not leave any fields blank.

It's really easy to get the latest information on any career field or industry. Go to this website, which lists free trade magazine subscriptions: www.freetrademagazinesource.com/.

Here's an example of how you could use a trade magazine. If you are interested in finding work in the area of making ice cream, look up trade magazines to get the latest information on ice cream technology. By subscribing to the *National Dipper* (www.nationaldipper.com) for free in exchange for your information, the *National Dipper* will send you the latest on ice-cream-making technology. You will also be able to read stories from small and large business owners in the ice-cream-making business. You will learn their names and then can start researching these companies for employment opportunities.

How about introducing yourself with, "Hello, Ms. Ice Cream Maker, my name is _____ and I was reading a very interesting article about you in *National Dipper magazine*." Do you think this person will then want to spend a few minutes listening to you continue with how brilliant the article was?

Trade Shows

Trade shows are also fantastic for getting next to people who are knowledgeable in your desired career area. At a trade show, thousands of people from all over the world typically show up to discuss, learn, and get new business. And so should you.

No matter how old you are, make sure you have a business card. (See the chapter on marketing yourself.) At trade shows, you can talk to lots of folks who have very specific knowledge about the industry or career sector. You can also observe how people in that field dress, talk, and present themselves. Often, there are free gifts and takeaways, as well as brochures chock full of information about the specific companies.

Carry yourself with some degree of confidence and do not let on you are there to find a job. You are attending to gain information and learn about what the wide selection of companies does and how they do it.

There are trade shows for everything—including ice cream. One major benefit of attending an ice cream show is the sheer amount of ice cream tasting that goes on! My personal favorite trade show was a sangria show at the convention center in San Juan, Puerto Rico.

Check out the list of trade shows in the United States on this website: https://www.expodatabase.com/trade-shows-america/usa/

Trade Associations

Join a trade association. In the United States alone, there are more than 7,800 trade associations for just about everything. Membership in a trade association costs money, but it is usually minimal.

Continuing with our ice cream example, there are several trade associations for ice cream, such as the National Ice Cream Retailers Association, the International Dairy Foods Association, and the Great Lakes Ice Cream & Fast Food Association, to name a few.

Why join an association? Being a member can get you the most up-to-date insider information and reveal trends in your chosen dream career. There is often a free newsletter or magazine for that specific industry that comes with your membership.

This is a powerful way to get ahead when looking for a job. Once you are a member, you can request a member list to find which organizations are listed. You will be able to get phone numbers, contacts, email addresses and more. Many times, magazines also have a classified section where job offers are announced. Plus, being a member of a trade association is nice to have on your resume. (More about this later.)

Business Publications

Local business journals are another great source for job leads and inside information on what's going on in your area. Business journals often have free trial subscriptions and can give you a heads up on things happening in any city.

Most business journals are also available for free online and offer great information, like new business filings and license applications.

Imagine beating everyone to the punch by contacting a business owner in your dream field directly, one day after she has filed for the new business. Use the opportunity to let her know you want to help her with her new business. Anyone opening a new business needs help. Make it easy for them. Check out https://en.wikipedia.org/wiki/Category:American_business_magazines

Construction Permits / New Construction Sites

Construction permits are published in business journals, online on your city's website, or at City Hall in print form. New business construction (for instance, if a company is expanding by adding a new building) can take time, but again it's about being in the right place at the right time. You can get the jump on everyone by being there first.

New Construction Sites

Visiting new construction sites is another great way to source a job. I don't recommend this to everyone, but it has worked for me selling phone systems. When I see a new construction site, I walk in like I own the place and look for posted construction permits. The post will have the owner's name and tenant. Then I ask one or more of the construction workers if they know when the project is to be completed. This will give you an idea of when you can get to work.

Job Fairs

Job fairs at colleges and universities provide additional opportunities to do research and get some great information about your desired field.

My personal experience is that you don't necessarily need to attend the school. Universities and colleges are public buildings and especially during public events like job fairs, no one asks for identification.

Get there early or as close to the opening time as possible. You will have less competition for meeting job recruiters. Bring business cards and a resume. Have fun, smile, shake hands, and find out who is there and what positions are available.

Large companies generally have booths or displays, but if you are lucky, smaller businesses may be there as well. You may even get to talk to a business owner. These are the ones who can make the hiring decision without having to send you to the Human Resources department.

Every participating company will have hand-outs and business cards. Send thank you notes to people who took the time to talk with you. Do your best to be memorable. (More about this later.)

Generally, no interviews take place at job fairs, which are more like speed dating. You and the company representatives are both looking for common ground. The following website provides a list of job fairs available nationwide:

www.employmentguide.com/job-fairs/browse

Using a few of these resources to research your dream job will provide you with a plethora of job leads. Remember, though, most great jobs are not advertised, they are found. More than ninety percent of people looking for jobs will not have considered going to a trade show or running down construction permits. Applying these techniques and doing your research will put you at the right place at the right time with the right information.

Try these affirmations:
1. I leave no stone unturned when looking for my dream job.
2. The Universe is conspiring to connect me with my dream job.
3. Someone is getting paid to eat ice cream for a living.

THINK LIKE AN ENTREPRENEUR

As a business owner, it's been my experience that some employees think there are endless amounts of money stockpiled in an offshore bank account under the employer's name. Nothing could be farther from the truth.

Have you ever been to Mexico or the south side of

Chicago? Everyone is selling something. There are fruit carts, clothing, hair braiding, jewelry, window washing, windshield-wiper-changing services, and my new personal favorite, stoplight street performers.

Everyone is an entrepreneur. To find a great job, you need to think like a business owner. Entrepreneurs provide products and services for pay. When looking for a job, take a page from our great president, John F. Kennedy, and ask not what your employer can do for you, but what you can do for your employer.

When interviewing, too many people make this mistake. It's not about what the company can do for you; it's about what you can do for them.

Business owners are optimistic chance-takers. They have to be. If they hear a good pitch that makes sense and it spreads the risk of doing business equally, why not give someone an opportunity to succeed?

This is how we entrepreneurs and business owners think. What we don't want to hear is how great you are, even though you might not have any direct experience, and how much you want to earn because you deserve it.

Entrepreneurs don't think this way. The best way to land your next dream job is by going into an interview, attending a trade show or networking event, and having an entrepreneurial mindset.

When you can explain what you can do, how well can you do it and present it in a way that is a low risk for the business owner, you are creating a win-win situation and will likely be able to land a job.

For example, try saying something like, "I would be willing to work on a ninety-day trial basis for only X amount of money. At the end of the ninety days, let's sit down and see if you can't live without me. If you can live without me, I will say thank you for the opportunity and head out the door."

This is the type of pitch a small business person wants to hear and one you should be saying if you want to get your foot in the door. Getting your foot in the door is the first step in building a career.

Let's recap:
- Think like an entrepreneur.
- Ask yourself what you can do for a company.
- Provide a win-win, no-strings-attached offer.
- When you get the job, be thankful every day.
- Ninety days is a short time to impress. Make the best of each and every day.

Try these affirmations:
1. I look at things through the mindset of a successful business owner.
2. I enter a job opportunity with an attitude that I deliver results.
3. I am grateful for every opportunity I have to learn and work.

MARKETING YOURSELF

Many people are already marketing themselves without even knowing it.

Trying to look good to attract that someone special? It's called marketing.

Having a Facebook page is a form of marketing yourself, too.

If you are looking for the right job, then marketing yourself properly can be a powerful tool, if used correctly. If done poorly, it can also have the opposite effect.

Marketing online has never been easier with tools like Facebook, LinkedIn, and Twitter. These can be great resources, but can also harm your efforts. For example, posting a picture of yourself doing a beer bong might get you written off as a potential job candidate.

Employers often check social media sites to get background information candidates might have left off their resumes.

Keep Facebook and other social media outlets personal. If you are serious, build career-based Facebook and LinkedIn pages that let people know you are a passionate, upstanding, and hard-working individual. You might impress that special someone with your new page.

Create Career Pages

A professional-looking career page should present you in a way that will impress a new employer. Get a professional photo taken and spell out areas of interest in your chosen career. Post good information that makes sense—and don't forget to spell-check and review before posting.

Link to companies with which you are interested in building your career. Invite people who can help further your career to "like" your page. It should go without saying that you shouldn't post party pictures and bad jokes.

A while back, my company placed an advertisement for a sales position. After receiving many resumes and applications, we checked out the Facebook pages of the ones with the most potential. One of the job hunters had a Facebook picture posted of her in a very bad light. Not good for her on many levels. Needless to say, we didn't hire her.

Let People Know You're Looking

Once you have established some good connections, let your contacts know you are looking for a new job. Oftentimes, a successful job search is about who you know.

Don't worry if you don't have the right contacts yet. Build a career page and keep posting to it. Including your Facebook and LinkedIn pages on a resume shows confidence and lets a prospective employer know you are serious.

Start a Blog

Starting your own blog is another easy way to market yourself. Blogging about your next career can help you better understand it, and could potentially connect you with the perfect position.

Creating a blog is not difficult and writing is very much like a muscle. The more you write and share your ideas, the easier it becomes. Potential employers will likely be very impressed if you can share your blog with them (make sure there are no typos and that your grammar is correct.)

Many companies lack the people, time, and know-how to do social media and regularly have old, outdated information on their websites.

There are limitless subjects to blog about. One of the topics could be your experience on finding a job in your chosen career.

Be sure to invite people to subscribe to your blog, especially anyone who has given you an interview. This will give you a chance to stay in touch with them so they can find out how brilliant you really are.

You can set up a free blog page at wordpress.com or even on Google. Include your new Facebook and LinkedIn pages on every email you send out. Include your Facebook, LinkedIn, and blog site on your business cards.

Business Cards

YES, business cards. Business cards are one of the least expensive ways of marketing yourself. Go to an office store and get fifty printed for ten dollars.

Why a business card? Because no one else being interviewed will have one and if you happen to meet someone outside of an interview, business cards are a great way to pass on your information.

A business card should be your mini-brochure with contact info and social media info. On the back side, add a list of your qualifications or services.

Remember, all you have to be is a little better than the next guy/girl to get the job. Having your own business card will say something about you. It says you are professional and organized. You will also need business cards for networking career events.

Networking

Networking career events? Yes, there are lots of them. Community colleges, universities, employers, chambers of commerce, and other job-finding organizations have them. These are typically advertised events that attract many employers.

Check out school websites and job placement areas. Don't worry if you did not go to the school. Networking events are easy to crash. You probably won't be talking to the business owner who can make a decision, but you may be able to get some great leads. Ask lots of questions at such events. This can produce tons of insight on what companies are seeking.

At my company, Telcom & Data, we usually attend two or three networking events a year. We are usually unimpressed with the level of motivation and enthusiasm some college students show at the events. At one job fair event at a local university, more than fifty companies were there to talk to prospective employees at 9 a.m. At our booth, no students showed up until closer to 11 a.m. It was a big room with hiring specialists just talking among themselves.

Have Your Own Private Networking Event

Sometimes you can have your own job networking event that only you know about. For example, every community has a chamber of commerce. The chambers often organize social events that encourage business owners and representatives to meet socially.

I have personally landed very significant business while standing in line at the snack bar. So can you. You typically don't have to be a member to go to an event and the costs are very nominal.

Go around, introduce yourself, get to know people, and above all, listen. Ask for business cards and take notes. The person you're speaking to might have valuable connections and know someone who can help you find your dream job.

At the very least, by attending such events, you become better at networking and meeting business people—for the most part, they are just regular people who work very hard and have a variety of interests.

I have met job seekers at chamber of commerce events and have a lot of respect for them. They are getting as close as possible to business owners and finding common ground to talk about. This shows they have initiative, one of the absolute best attributes to have.

These are the people I want to surround myself with. People can be trained to do a job, but you can't teach initiative and enthusiasm. I have personally seen jobs go to people just because someone liked them.

Remember to send an email to everyone you meet, telling them it was nice connecting with them and invite them to subscribe to your blog.

Build your network and keep going to different events even when you have found your dream job.

Volunteering

Volunteering will help you get a job. If you're not working right now, find a volunteer job. Volunteering can considerably raise your chances of landing a job.

There are so many places that need help and could use your skills and support. Volunteering can help you make great connections, provide you with valuable experience and free training, make your resume look a whole lot better and help you feel good. Helping always puts a positive twist on things.

Your 30-Second Elevator Pitch

You are in an elevator and a business owner strikes up a conversation. You realize you want to work for her company and only have two minutes. What do you say? You need to get to the point but provide enough information to spark her interest and to sound unique. Not as easy as it sounds, but you need this.

Make your elevator pitch powerful, intriguing, and sincere. Start with an opening statement that gets the other person listening.

How about a question? For example, "Do you think most people are doing what they are really passionate about?"

Wait for the answer and connect to something the other person says. You can then continue, "I am passionate about _____ . My goal is to work with an entrepreneur who shares this same passion. This would create a powerful synergy to really get things moving for both of us."

Then, if the opportunity seems to be one to pursue, list your drive, eagerness to learn and dedication to reaching your goals.

Write your own elevator pitch. It comes in handy when you know you only have a few seconds to impress someone. Be flexible and change parts of it, depending on who you are talking to. Practice it and own it. It is yours.

Educate Yourself on the Cheap

Learn as much as you can about your desired career

area. There is so much free or almost-free training and education available today, it's amazing. My personal favorites are online webinars, seminars, or free product training. Many companies offer free webinars so you don't even have to leave your house.

This type of training is done by leading experts so what you end up learning is the latest information available. All you need is a computer, smartphone and your imagination.

Why do companies offer free training? They want to sell their products. The way they sell them is by training people on how the products or services work. These types of seminars are available for virtually any industry and career you can think of.

Need an example? A friend of mine is a DJ who, after getting married, started to look for work he could do during the day. He has been a DJ in Chicago for the last ten years and knows lots of club owners.

Through one of my contacts, I found out about a job opening at a company that sells high-end sound systems and suggested that my friend get in touch with the manufacturer. I also suggested he get some free training.

Looking online, I found out that there was a free three-day seminar being put on by another manufacturer. The seminar covered everything and even included free breakfast and lunch, and was being held at a very nice upscale hotel. My friend was able to take what he learned as a DJ and apply the seminar training to get into a new career. For FREE!

Here is a short list I compiled simply by looking on the Internet for seminars in the city of Milwaukee. Use keywords in your search that are in your dream career.

- Automotive Seminar:
    Free Automotive Painting Seminar
    Free 2-night seminar
- Web Designer: Free Seminar Introduction into HTML and Page Layout
- Esthetician Seminar Milwaukee

Please keep in mind that you will sometimes need to change keyword search terms, for example, *wholesale, supplier, manufacturer seminar*. If you can't find anything in your city, expand your search to regional or state or nationwide search. Think like a business owner.

Trade shows are another great way of getting free or almost-free training. Trade shows offer intense, two- to five-day events with classes being held all day long. Registering for a show is easy. Just use a company name, address, and email. As I mentioned above, every profession and industry offers a trade show.

Try these affirmations:
1. I am my own brand.
2. I market myself as an awesome business opportunity to everyone I meet.
3. Who couldn't use my awesome services?

Your Resume

Resumes are the most boring thing ever. But for you, the best branded, marketed job seeker ever, your resume is only a menu of your services and experiences. Your resume has about five seconds to get the reader's attention.

You need to make sure that your resume is error free with no misspellings, and with correct grammar and easy-to-read fonts. An excellent resource for resume development is the University of Arizona. *__https://eller.arizona.edu/programs/undergraduate/professional-development/career-preparation/resume-cover-letter__*

I would spend more time on a custom introduction letter then a resume. Remember, you are not a person who is emailing resumes in the hope of getting a job. You are a butt-kicking job seeker who is knocking on doors and meeting people face-to-face to get your dream job.

A cover letter is custom and personal. It is specific to the owner of the business you want to work for. The more you know about a company you want to work for, the better the cover letter.

There are some excellent examples of cover letters:

Virgin Corporation
Sir Richard Branson

Dear Sir Richard Branson,

Thank you in advance for your time. After careful consideration I am certain that your company and vision is perfectly suited for our mutual success. Like you, I also have a driving passion for making the world a better place through better technology and services. I write to you specifically because I believe we have much in common and I would be great at helping you create a worldwide entrepreneurial vehicle that could help youth and business owners to improve employment opportunities. This program would teach young job seekers and businesses how to think in terms of mutual respect and successful outcomes. The program would reach young job seekers in events held at high schools and would call on local personalities in music, sports and leadership to deliver inspired messages before the lively seminar that asks tough, rhetorical questions about the future and reveals a different option of going after the job of your dreams and entrepreneurship.

I believe this idea is a perfect fit for your vast experience and contacts and together we could deliver a powerful program that inspires both youth and business owners.

Applying for Your Dream Job

Getting your dream job is all about knocking on the right door.

The most effective way to do it is to knock on the door of the place you want to work—at small to medium-sized companies. This approach does not work well for large corporations, which generally have a more formal application process.

The idea of knocking on the door is to talk to the owner directly. From your research, you will know that person's name. If you can't find the owner's name on the company's website, check out www.manta.com, which has profiles of millions of businesses.

Knock on the door and be as confident as possible. You have been practicing. Ask for Mr. or Ms. _____. If there is a receptionist who asks who you are, offer your business card and state your name in a clear, confident voice.

If the receptionist asks why you would like to see Mr. / Ms. _____, tell the recep-tionist it is personal and that you need five minutes of Mr./Ms. _____ time.

If the receptionist says the person is busy, ask if there is a time you can come back and set up an appointment. If the receptionist digs deeper as to why you are here, offer up, "I am not selling anything," and emphasize that you only need five minutes of the boss's time. Typically when you persevere, you will prevail.

THE INTERVIEW

There are two kinds of interviews—the ones that go well and the ones that don't. The ones that don't go well are usually because they were not properly planned. Having a good interview is not a hard thing- it's just honest and open communication.

The best candidate I ever experienced as a business owner actually had more questions for me than I did for him. The job applicant interviewed me, and because he had so many good questions, it was clear he had done his research on my company. He called former employees to gain insight. He knew everything about us. That was very impressive; so much so that he ended up getting the job.

Doing research on a company is easier than ever. Look at the company's website and check out the "About Us" (or equivalent) page. Check search engines for news regarding the compa-ny. Look for press releases the company may have published. Check out similar companies in the area that may be competitors of the company you are interested in working for.

REALLY IMPORTANT! Put together a list of ten to twenty questions to bring to an interview. The more the better. Practice asking the questions.

Want to be a great dancer? Practice.

Want to play golf well? Practice.

Want to play piano and amaze your friends? Practice.

Want to get a job? Practice. Practice in front of the

mirror, practice on your dog, or practice with a friend. Practice makes perfect.

How to DRESS

What should you wear to an interview? I can't believe we have to have to talk about this, but we do. When I was about twenty years old, I studied fashion at the Chicago Fashion Institute. I went there because I thought my dream job would be in fashion.

However, the most important thing I learned there was that fashion matters when it comes to making that first impression, especially on first dates and interviews.

When showing up to an interview, the minimum for men is a crisp, well-ironed shirt, tie, pressed pants, and polished shoes. Nothing—and I mean nothing—else will do. I have seen people who literally rolled out of bed in the clothes they slept in and show up for a job fair.

Don't know how to tie a tie? Go online or ask your next door neighbor if you need help. I don't care if your dream job is garbage collector, butcher, or auto mechanic—appearances and first impressions matter.

Believe it or not, ladies, both young and not-so-young, can dress inappropriately for a job interview. I once had a woman in her autumn years show up in a fur jacket with a tight, short skirt and stiletto heels. When I offered to hang up her jacket, she revealed an amazingly low-cut blouse that showed off more than necessary.

When I asked what position she was applying for, she said she had just lost her job as an executive assistant to a high-powered attorney who had just retired. I asked again what she was applying for and she said, "Anything you need me for, but something that pays more than 50K per year." I thought to myself, "Wow, she actually lost her dream job."

I also interviewed an intern who showed up in yoga pants. Really? Yes, really. I asked her to go back home and come back wearing attire for an interview. She did.

The minimum for ladies is a crisp blouse, blazer, and a skirt or dress slacks. Don't wear black because black is more associated with party clothes and of course don't wear your party clothes, either. Remember, if you don't have money for new clothing, there is always Goodwill.

Whether you're male or female, there are also organizations that can help you dress for success for free or next to nothing. Check out:

- Dress for Success, www.dressforsuccess.org/
- Career Gear, www.careergear.org/
- Diva-Divo, www.diva-divo.org/

Meeting the Boss

OK, you've got your interview questions and look smooth in your interview threads. Let's go meet the boss.

The boss needs help. Say it again. *THE BOSS NEEDS HELP!* It is your responsibility to make him/her understand you are not here only to collect a check, but are applying for the position to help the company make more money and get them more time with their family. Bottom line, that is what every entrepreneur or boss wants.

You can do this! The boss is a person, too. He or she might be curious as to who you are and why you want to meet.

Now is the time. When the owner comes and you get to meet your new boss, smile, shake the person's hand firmly, and look him/her straight in the eye and say, "Hello, Mr/Ms _____, My name is _____. It's a pleasure to meet you. Thank you for taking a few minutes to meet with me."

When the boss leads you into his/her office or conference room, take note of things. Are there more questions that come to your mind?

Once a meeting room has been determined, do not take a seat until the new boss sits down. This is a subtle show of respect. I once met a customer who was from Germany and he shook my hand, bowed, and clicked his boot heels together. When I looked down, I saw beautifully polished boots. Was I impressed!

If you are in a conference room, you are at a slight disadvantage compared to being in the boss's office. Don't sit far away from the boss or on the other side of the conference room table. Old friends don't sit far away. Sit down right next to the boss and ever so slightly, mimic his or her movements. If the boss folds his or her hands, fold your hands. If the boss leans back in the chair, then sit back yourself.

Hopefully, you are actually going to meet in the boss's

office, because often there are personal effects on display. It's like walking into someone's house for the first time.

Look around and learn. What does this person like? Check out the furniture, pictures, trophies, awards—the more the better. These items provide you with an ice-breaker. Ask about anything you see.

For example, in my office, I have two guitars and two sets of golf clubs, as well as pictures of my family. It might be obvious, but asking me if I play guitar would be a good ice-breaker.

A salesman was once in my office and asked if I played. He said that he did as well, so I showed him a new guitar I had just purchased. Then we both started to play. Now that was a great ice-breaker. We became buddies before he went into his sales pitch.

Now go into your pitch. It could be something like this. "I am here because I want to help you ... plant corn, change tires, walk dogs, taste ice cream, repair houses, do photography, grill, barbecue (or whatever your dream job is)...and would like an opportunity to work specifically for your company. I have done some research on your company and I (have experience or don't have experience). I have the best potential to help you grow your business in any way I can. I would like to share with you why working here would be my dream job."

Then state five quick facts about the company. For instance, "I know that your company was founded in XXXX and you have had very good success with (list products or services). I know that you are ... expanding, moving, getting into a new area, competing, or anything else you can found out about the company when you did your research.)

Then ask this question. "Do you remember when you were starting out and you were looking for that one chance to prove yourself? Someone gave you that chance. Otherwise you would not be here today. I am looking for that same chance and I know it can work because I am passionate about what you do here at NAME OF COMPANY. Can you provide a spot on your team for me?" OR "I would like this to be a win-win situation and I don't want you to take all the risk. That's why I propose a ninety-day trial. My job will be to show you that I'm exactly who I say I am. If after ninety days you are not completely thrilled with my performance, just tell me. I will thank you and walk out the door without going to unemployment."

After the Interview

I am always amazed at how little follow-up goes on after a prospective job seeker sends in his or her resume. It's as though applicants think that being hired depends solely on their resume.

When my company places an advertisement seeking help, I always include the phrase, "We don't hire resumes."

What would that mean to you?

Apparently, not a lot of people understand that the resume is not what gets them hired.

Following up on a resume is really important and shows you are serious about the job.

How to Follow Up

Following up should always be done at least three times. Notice the words *at least*?

First, follow up right after an interview. Send a thank you email thanking the boss for his or her time. Include any positive details or commonalities you may have discussed. When considering a new hire, the successful candidate often will be the one who is memorable. Be memorable by sending a thank you note that reminds the boss of why you are too good to pass up.

Second, send a letter. Emails are often ignored or accidentally deleted without reading them. An envelope with a handwritten address will get opened. (If you have poor handwriting, get someone who has great penmanship and get that person to address the envelope for you.) Include a typed letter recapping all of your abilities and enthusiasm for working at that company. You can also include a newspaper or printed online article about something relevant to the business and comment about it. Make sure whatever you are sending is really relevant.

Remember, the idea is to stay in the mind of the boss, who likely gets lots of calls and emails. However, a personal letter is rare and memorable.

Third, follow up with a phone call. Staying in touch will help your chances of landing a job. Any entrepreneur understands and appreciates persistence. I know I do. When calling, don't be bashful or nervous. The purpose of this call is to get your foot in the door.

A follow-up call might go like this, "Hello, Ms./Mr. _____, this is _____ (your name). Is this a good time to talk?"

Wait until the boss says yes or no. If it's no, then schedule another time that's convenient for the boss. If it's yes, then continue.

"I've been thinking about our meeting and more than ever, I am convinced I need to get my foot in the door with your organization. I know it's sometimes difficult to bring in people and to take a chance, but I assure you that when someone is as determined as I am to have that opportunity to work in their dream field, no matter where I start, I can promise I won't blow it for us both. It's not about the money; it's about the opportunity to work for your company. Even if I have to start from the bottom, would you be able to find a place on your team's roster for me?"

Don't say anything after you ask the boss for the job. If he or she says yes, be prepared to thank your new boss with as much enthusiasm as possible.

If the boss says no, thank him/her for the time and consideration. Remember, "no" doesn't necessarily mean "no" forever. Ask if would be okay to check back in a month or two. Usually, the answer will be yes.

I have hired people I said "no" to and then hired them because they called when I really needed help.

At every company, there is always someone who is taking their job, boss, fellow employees, or customers for granted. They show up late, drop the ball and don't really care. All you have to do is be better than that person and be diligent and patient.

If you REALLY want to work for a specific company, stay in touch. Even if you get another job, let them know you are working, but still have your eye on working for them.

You can and you will get your dream job!

I DIDN'T GET THE JOB. NOW WHAT?

So you did everything right. You researched your job. Fantasized about working there. Walked in with your business card, smile, and firm handshake. You wrote down all of your questions and reasons on why you would be a great addition to the company and on top of that shined your shoes, fixed your hair, and the boss still said NO?

Get over it. Remember, even the best hitters in baseball get to base three out of ten times.

I have failed hundreds of times. I have spent years working with a customer only to get denied at the last minute. Landing your dream job is not a sprint, but a marathon. What you do next will set you apart from the rest of the job seekers out there.

The next step? *Be grateful.*

You just came really close. You walked into your Dream Job and hopefully talked with the owner. Now you need to follow up. This is what separates the mere wannabes from the professionals. If you are getting denied in person, be grateful and thank the boss for his or her time. Ask the boss if there are things you can work on that could help you the next time you ask for a job.

What the boss or the person interviewing you tells you might be surprising. Thank them and ask them if they would please keep your resume and business card in case things change. (Things always do.)

Also ask them if they know of a business associate who might need help, and if so, would they please pass on your resume, or better yet, please take a copy so they can keep one and have one to pass on.

Let the person know that you will be hard at work learning more about your Dream Job.

Why is this important? Two reasons:

1. Gratitude gets you in the right frame of mind.
2. Remember when I said you only have to be better than their worst person? Things change. The boss can instantly be fed up with a person who is lazy, late, sloppy, and uncaring. Also, if you were competing against another job candidate, make sure to send a thank you card.

A high percentage of new hires don't work out. (They should have read this book.) If someone who is hired ahead of you doesn't work out, you can be in a great position to get back in for another interview, if you were memorable.

Because you were grateful and memorable, the interviewer might mention you to a busi-ness associate who needs help. Business owners often socialize and the number one complaint we all share is how hard it is to find the right people.

Stay in touch with your Dream Job opportunity by stopping by, dropping an email, and using Google Alerts to keep track of any news about the company. As soon as you hear an update or positive message, pounce on it with an email or phone call. The boss will wonder why none of the current employees are as excited about the good news as you are. This move will prove you are paying attention. It will also indicate that the company needs someone like you on their team.

* * * * *

Now it's time to practice even more than ever. You had a taste of calling on a business owner, and it would be good to polish your approach. Spend more time practicing your pitch in front of the mirror or with family members. It takes something like ten thousand hours practicing to become an expert.

Lastly, if you don't succeed, start focusing on your next opportunity. Don't stop until you open another door, and another. You will succeed once you drop the stories you have been telling yourself about why you can't, and turn them into why you can.

You are perfect for your Dream Job. Be memorable and always be grateful.

Now let's get to work!

I GOT MY JOB! NOW WHAT?

First, let me congratulate you for your success! Well done!

18 Things to Help Make You Indispensable at Your New Job

1. **Never wait around to do another task.** If you have competed a task or have nothing to do, find something or ask someone. You never want to get caught slacking off. Never slack off.

I once fired a guy because he was sitting in a chair with his eyes closed, head phones plugged in, listening to music. I asked him what he was doing, and he said he had finished the task at hand and since I was not around to TELL him to do the next thing, he was "waiting" for me. Wrong answer. Use your imagination and never slack off.

2. **Get to the office early.** Start the coffee.
3. **Clean up the kitchen area.** Any dirty cups in the sink? Clean them. I don't care if you don't drink coffee. You're the new person. Help out anyway you can.

4. **Keep a candy jar filled by your desk and let everyone know they can help themselves.** Having people stop by to get a sugar fix gives you an opportunity to find out what's going on and what projects they are working on. Maybe you can help.

5. **Volunteer to do things.** Take detailed notes at meetings and anytime they need someone to do a task, like go to the store, jump on it with enthusiasm. Be the best "go-fer" ever.

6. **Sign up for free training.** With so much new technology available, there are lots of free training and online certifications. Find out how you can take these classes, which are almost always free.

   For example, there may be an online video on how to operate the phone system. Take it. The same goes for the postage machine, any technology around the office, tools, software, computers, or anything that can help make you the go-to person inside the office.

   I keep saying office, but it can be anywhere your dream job takes you.

7. **Go above and beyond.** Be above and beyond anyone's expectations. For example, if it's snowing outside, get out there and brush off others people's cars. It shows you care and that you are a genuinely nice person. Or perhaps you got to work early, so you shoveled the path. Do

anything you can think of.

8. **Find a task that no one likes to do and own it.** I used to volunteer at my kids' school for Friday night fish fry in the kitchen. I had clean-up duty. There was one job no one wanted to do, which was to clean out the grease from the fryers. Then came a young lady who had worked in her parent's restaurant as a kid.

   Guess what she had to do? She was an ace at it. She never worked Friday nights. Instead, she came in over the weekend at her convenience and cleaned the fryer with pride. Hats off to her and to you if you can find that one task.

9. **Always say, "Yes, sir" and "No, ma'am."** I know that's not how most kids talk today, but I don't care; respect is timeless."Saying "Yes, sir" and "No, ma'am" to everyone shows respect and gets you respect. Never miss an opportunity.

10. **Offer to bring back lunch if you are going out.** Make it your thing. Say you are going to that great sandwich shop around the corner. Let other people in the office know you are going and ask if you can bring back something for them. People love this, especially if the weather is bad.

11. **Actually, this should be number one on the list.** Be grateful for your job and everyone who is showing you the ropes. Be very thankful to everyone everywhere, not just at work. I am grateful you are reading this.

12. **Offer to help cover for employees who are on vacation or out sick.** This can get you better insight on other tasks and jobs. This is the way to the top. Let me know when you get there.

13. **Offer to write or to become a regular contributor to the company's website, blog, or Facebook page.** So many companies forget to constantly update information. The boss will love this one.

14. **Be the most positive person at the company, as well you should, because it's your dream.** Who better to be happy? Being a positive person gives off good vibrations. Positive people attract positive people. Smile at everyone and say "Good morning" with enthusiasm. Not your style? Practice in the mirror!

15. **Answer the phone in the same mind-blowing positive manner.** I have all of my employees answer the phone the same way. "It's a great day at Telcom & Data. This is _____ How may I help you?"

    You have to say it with a smile. A person the other side of the phone can sense a smile. When the boss starts hearing about this person who is blowing customers away with this great phone greeting, it will be mandatory.

    It is a great day, isn't it?

16. **At my company, we get lots of magazines and no one straightens them out or gets rid of old ones.** Help keep the area tidy and I will be grateful.

17. **Make it a habit to be helpful, thankful, appreciative, positive, and enthusiastic.** This will make it easy for others around you to help teach you what they know. On the other hand, if you lack energy, are lazy, or boring, or not very helpful yourself, then why on earth would anyone want to help you? Get the right attitude and people will bend over backwards for you.

18. **It does not matter where you start with your dream job.** If you are only sweeping the floors, you can learn. Be forever grateful of the broom because it holds the key to your success. Keep smiling and keep your eye on the big picture.

ABOUT THE AUTHOR

Author, speaker, and Telcom & Data CEO Ricardo Trinidad has been an entrepreneur as long as he can remember. Raised in a working-class family on Chicago's South Side, his Puerto Rican father and Texan mother led by example through their daily hard work. Trinidad followed suit, "making" jobs for himself to earn extra money.

After completing high school and a few college courses, Trinidad's path led to the telecommunications industry. Employed by an Edison, NJ-based telecom and data company, he was asked to open an office in Chicago. After a few years, Trinidad founded Telcom & Data in his Chicago apartment with three thousand dollars in savings.

His risk and tenacity paid off. The company grew quickly because of his industry knowledge, the relationships he had built in the field, and his collaborative leadership style.

Twenty-two years later and now headquartered in Milwaukee, Telcom & Data is one of the nation's leading providers of traditional telecommunications equipment.

Trinidad is a sought-after speaker and trainer who particularly enjoys mentoring young people.

LinkedIn:
/ricardotrinidad